Tracing Your Roots

Tracing Your Roots

Locating Your Ancestors Through Landscape and History

Meg Wheeler

TIGER BOOKS INTERNATIONAL
LONDON

This edition published in 1996 by
Tiger International PLC, Twickenham
ISBN 1-85501-845-4

This book was designed and produced by Todtri Productions Limited
P.O. Box 572, New York, NY 10116-0572 FAX: (212) 279-1241

Printed and bound in Singapore

Author: Meg Wheeler

Publisher: Robert M. Tod
Designer and Art Director: Ron Pickless
Editor: Nicolas Wright
Typeset and DTP: Blanc Verso/UK

Understanding
a Family's Past

Opposite top: Enlistment poster from World War 1 dated 1915 - these patriotic posters were everywhere, encouraging young men to join up and fight for King and Country.

Opposite below: Action at the French Front in World War 1.

Below: The Complete Carter Clan - group family picture taken c.1910 showing James Jabez born 1840 and his wife Emma, their nine children and spouses, six grandchildren and two great-grandchildren outside the row of cottages where they lived in the newly drained Fens of East Anglia, England.

Everyone has roots, somewhere. The search for these roots may be long and can be difficult but must surely bring the highest reward of satisfaction and self-knowledge. Not only are new friendships made, but family kinships cemented all over the world. No matter where you are living at the moment, there are ways to find out about your earlier family history, often no further away than your local library.

The earliest civilisations, whether they were the Egyptians, the Romans, the Incas or the Greeks, each influenced later peoples, leaving behind traces of their lives in both the physical sense and the genealogical sense. Each one of us can trace some part of our physical attributes back to earlier times, regardless of colour, creed or race. It is simply a matter of unravelling the strands of time and following carefully.

Why do so many people want to find out about their family history? Perhaps it has something to do with the changes in society within the past century. One hundred years ago the family unit was, on the surface, far more stable than today. The men went out to work, the women stayed home to care for the children and provide a home for the men. Elderly parents and grandparents were cared for by the family, and older children often took responsibility for the infants, thus spreading the load for the mother. Many people find that the only way to cope with the stress of modern life and the calculated hardness of the world today is by knowing their own roots and being able to draw from the depth of family continuity, of knowing that

Above and right: Women at war work.

Opposite top: Serried ranks of war graves - Commonwealth War Graves Commission Cemetery, Etaples in France which served the nearby military hospital where the wounded and dying from both sides of World War 1 were taken. Here can be found memorials for every nation involved including non- combatents such as drivers, stretcher-bearers, musicians and nurses.

Opposite below: Gone, but Not Forgotten - typical memorials to fallen soldiers of World War 1 from Canadian Cemetery, France.

others in their family faced such adversity in years long past.

The delving into a family's past or family history is becoming an increasingly popular pastime. Societies and local groups meet regularly to offer help and advice to beginners, books and magazines abound and there are even dedicated software programmes for the computer enthusiast to both record and print out family histories.

The pursuit of your family history soon highlights the fundamental changes that have taken place in our society, all over the world, in the last 100 years.

The advent of World War I in 1914 not only destroyed many millions of men's lives by either killing them outright or maiming them, but also liberated the women who had been called upon to do the men's work whilst they were away fighting. No longer were they tied to the home and hearth but could compete in the market place for jobs previously felt to be exclusively the preserve of men. This Great War was the first really global conflict, evidenced by the serried ranks of gravestones in War Cemeteries such as that at Etaples in France where may be found the graves for Chinese, Jewish, British, Irish, Australian, German, Indian and other nationalities of all ranks.

Over the last century advances in science and technology meant more work became available, education improved and children leav-

Opposite: General George Armstrong Custer (1839-1876) taken c.1865 - famous for his Last Stand at Little Bighorn. Family legends may mention involvement in similar military action.

Right: King Edward VII, then Prince of Wales, with Queen Alexandra and their sons and daughters.

Below: Beautiful example of bound Family Bible inside which may well be recorded details of marriages, births of children and burials of family members.

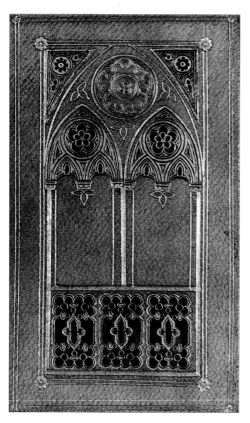

Right: George Washington crossing the Delaware - were your ancestors on the winning side of this campaign?

ing school were able to work for increasingly higher wages, enabling them to set up their own homes away from their immediate family. Families slowly split up, divided not only by physical distance but also by psychological distance, the gap between the generations widened with parents and grandparents remembering times when the family stayed together and the children wanting a new independence.

The family home has certainly not been immune from these changes. All over the world, there has been a continuous, steady drift away from the country into towns and cities. As the old housing tenements and slums created by this migration were cleared and new modern housing took their place, old familiar landmarks were bull-dozed away and new townscapes emerged. Motor cars and aero-

Battle of Bunker's Hill 1775 - American War of Independence. One of the more famous battles in this bitter war between Great Britain and the colonies of America. Family legends may lead back to this or other similar campaigns when settlers had to choose between their past and their future.

Opposite: The English General Cornwallis surrenders to Washington at Yorktown, American War of Independence 1781.

Carlton House, Upwood in Huntingdonshire, England - ancient timber-frame house built in 1600s, details of which appear in local printed records. Sir Oliver Cromwell, uncle of the famous Oliver Cromwell of English Civil War fame, lived in the Manor House overlooking this house and may well have dined there.

planes gave instant access to distant places, children moved away to follow careers and grandchildren, instead of being constantly under foot, became a rare treat on short visits. The habit of talking, story telling and exchanging gossipy news is slowly dying out within families, split apart in a modern world and, with this distancing, many family stories are also being forgotten. With divorce becoming common in many societies, children are loosing touch with separated parents, thus missing out on part of their family heritage. The art of letter writing has been replaced with the quick telephone call.

For many of us the urge to trace our roots comes suddenly. The passing of an elderly relative, the birth of a new member to the family or the marriage of a child suddenly awakens an interest in preserving the past to hand on to the future. It may be the unexpected inheritance, a family bible, a mourning ring or a book of family portraits that triggers the need to know more. Family stories and legends of historic deeds, voyages of adventure or, perhaps, misadventure can all fuel the fire of curiosity. Pride in national or cultural heritage or in a family name can create a desire to preserve the family history in writing. Other people may have long had the desire to find out more about their families but had neither the time nor the knowledge.

Whatever the reason for wishing to record a family history, the basic skills are universal.

Imagine the thrill of discovering your great-great grandfather was with Custer at Little Big Horn or fought at the Alamo. Which side did your family take in the American Civil War, did they fight with Ulysses S. Grant or Robert E. Lee? Were they on the First Fleet to Australia? Did they stand for King or Parliament in the English Civil War of 1640, did they volunteer to help Francis Drake fight the invasion threat from the Spanish Armada in 1588? Upon which ever side of the Atlantic you now live, whose side would your ancestors have taken in the American War of Independence 1776-1783?

The records containing information on our ancestors abound, ranging from church, taxation and civil records back to wills and early property deeds. In these records it is possible to find out not only when an ancestor was born, married and buried but also what sort of clothes they wore, the food they ate, the newspapers they read and the people they would have met in the local market square and inn.

Whether your interest is in a particular family line, a family name or an historical house, the records exist to help you find out more. In the following chapters, different sources for this information are explained, where to find them and how to interpret them.

The main requirements for successfully tracing your family roots must be curiosity, determination, patience and a good measure of luck. No additional skills or equipment are required and a minimum of cost is involved.

Running Account for Fellowes Estate, Ramsey in Huntingdonshire dated 1807 - a good example of the detailed information available about the work our ancestors did and how much they were paid. Most of the work was manual labour - cutting wood, mending fences and casting up manure to be used as fertiliser.

17

First Steps

S o how do you start to trace your roots. Perhaps the most important resource that everyone has is their own memory. In order to find out more about a family's history, it is essential to start at the beginning - yourself. Where possible, talk with your relatives, bring out the family albums and recall holidays, marriages, births and even funerals. Many folk have a keepsake box or drawer into which they put all their treasures - newspaper cuttings of weddings, baptisms and obituaries; important events in their lives - receiving an award, a medal or meeting with a famous personality. There may even be original birth certificates, marriage certificates, funeral cards and possibly death certificates as well as address books, birthday books and even diaries. With care, photographs of family gatherings can be copied and the names of the people written on the copy for ease of reference. The originals can then be stored safely.

Many older relatives are only too pleased to talk about their youth, people they knew and places they visited. They may not remember exact dates but it is usually easy to deduce these from other local or national events, such as wars, elections, fairs or important family events. A tape recorder is very useful for recording con-

Typical family heirloom - a group photograph dated c.1900 showing parents with nine children. Note the blur made by the baby moving - these early portrait pictures may seem stiff and posed but everyone had to remain very still for a long time.

versations, hearing the same story told from two or more different viewpoints can highlight discrepancies and confirm facts. Make a note of any family legends or any areas that are avoided since these may be worth investigating further. If your family were immigrants and settled in your country, try to find out as much as possible about the 'homeland' especially the date of arrival and place of settlement. All of these treasured mementoes can add to the knowledge of the immediate family and may be linked up with heirlooms such as family Bibles and printed pedigrees.

Local Sources

A library is the first place to visit when looking for local information. Not only will you find out more about the area but also learn what national records are available locally. Look out especially for county histories published by the state or county. Newspapers and periodicals, often on microfilm, which may give details of local events, notices of birth, marriage and death as information on immigrant arrivals, obituaries of prominent local citizens and religious group meetings.

Entry from the Autograph Book of Miss Rose Collett of Ellenhall, Staffordshire in England. Each floral surround was hand-painted by Rose. Family members and close friends wrote a message, often dated, inside the nosegay. Such autograph books can give invaluable family information as well as being collectable.

Original short-form Birth Certificate for Horace Cyril Carter born 27th February 1914. They were issued free-of-charge when registering a birth, payment being required for the full birth certificate showing details of parents. Many folk did not feel it necessary to pay the extra and therefore only this short-form survives.

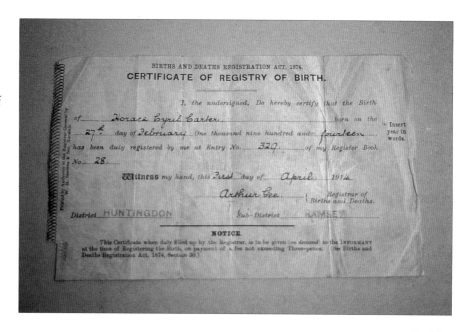

Beautiful sampler dated 1868 made by Elizabeth Graystone of Exeter in England. Such examples of needlework were produced by young girls as proof of their sewing skills and the custom dates back many centuries. Many are now valued heirlooms, framed and put on display.

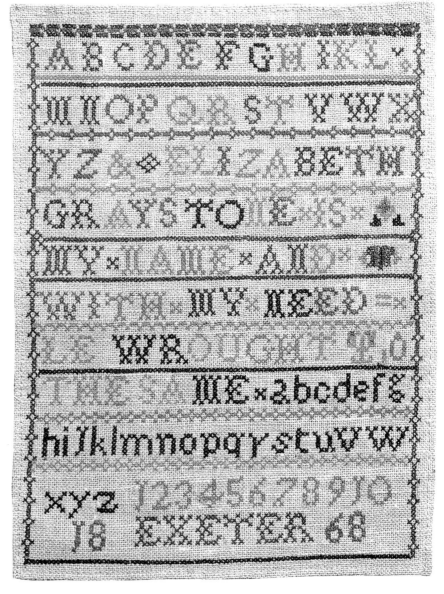

More importantly, this will be the place to find research manuals such as the American *Handy Book for Genealogists* which lists each state in America, giving a brief history with a map and the address of the county clerk who holds the early land records together with birth, marriage and death records amongst other archives. Similar publications such as *In Search of European Roots* and *In Search of German Roots* (both available in Canada) and the *Bibliography of Loyalist Source Materials in Archives in the United States, Canada and Great Britain* give vital information on available records and where to find them.

The series of *Victoria County Histories for Great Britain* are particularly useful for researching English county history. Each parish within a county is described with details of the history of the church and village or town and the names of the landowners. Also look out for trade directories that commence in the 1840s and give detailed information, county by county, of tradespeople and gentry.

In many cases a knowledge of the geographical area is essential as

Collage of family heirlooms - a typical collection of treasured family mementoes such as might be found in any family chest, including memorial cards, family photographs, original birth and marriage certificates, letters and newspaper cuttings.

Opposite: A settler and his wife in North Carolina c.1903. For many people, the building of a home and clearing of the land was back-breaking work. Many gave up the struggle and moved into towns, but those pioneers who persevered reaped the rewards.

Left: John Smith (1580-1631) the famous pioneer in the British colonies of North America. Best known for his marriage with Pocahontas, the native North American Indian princess. The biographies of such explorers and early settlers have usually been recorded and can be found in most large lending libraries.

Below: Entries in a small Family Bible showing birth dates for members of the Cox family of Ramsey, Huntingdonshire in England. This family were staunch Methodists and none of the children were baptised in the Parish Church, so this record of births in the mid-1800s is invaluable for the family history.

well as the language spoken. In Canada and America the spread of settlement from the coastal areas inland resulted in the formation of new states and counties and the movement of families can be traced by the growth pattern of the area. Electoral Rolls, some of which date back to the mid 1800s, will also give vital information on a family location and can be used to plot the time of arrival in a particular place.

Australia is particularly well catered for with many publications available from lending libraries and found on the shelves in the reference sections. These books cover the initial settlement of the continent and include such well known titles as *The First Fleeters* recording details of the first shipments of convicts to Australia from England.

If your family roots are in a foreign country, try to learn as much as possible about that country, it's history, language and customs.

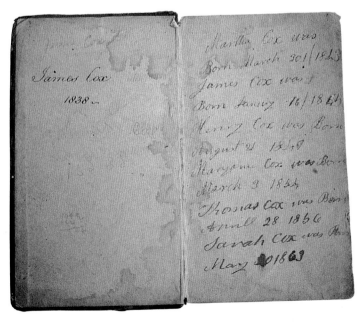

Heraldic devices dating from mid-1800s. Only direct descendants of those to whom the original grant of arms was made are entitled to display a coat of arms. Each shield contains coded information on the families represented and a record of all grants made is held by the appropriate authority.

Printed Histories

Many of the early families who settled in the Americas, Australia and New Zealand have been recorded in printed reference books. New books are constantly being published giving listings of names taken from shipping lists and immigration records covering later periods. Certainly the early settlers in America have mostly been recorded and many Americans can proudly trace their descent from these early pioneers. Three of the most well-known of these reference books for American settlement are by J C Hoten, C E Banks and P C Coldham, all available from libraries and genealogical societies. They give details of early settlers, their families and the date of arrival in America and, in some cases, the destination within the new country.

Australian researchers have produced a wealth of material on their

Knights in armour c.1500. Note that even the horses have protective armour. Such a knight would weigh many pounds and if unhorsed would be at a great disadvantage, unable to move about easily. Therefore the horses needed protection as well as the knight.

Gravestone embedded in wall of Parish Church, Porlock in Somerset, England. This example of an 18th-century gravestone shows Joane wife of William Brown died in 1779 aged 57 years and William Brown died in 1786 aged 75 years. Such information would prove a most helpful starting point for anyone tracing that family.

early settlers, many of whom were convicts from British gaols whose families may have travelled out with them as free-born settlers. Amongst the best known is *The Founders of Australia - a Biographical Dictionary of the First Fleet* by Mollie Gillen.

Settlers in South Africa have produced *The Settler Handbook* which describes the 1820 settlers from the UK to South Africa in detail, published by Chameleon Press of Capetown.

Canadians should look out for locally produced biographies. Loyalist guides such as *Loyalists of Ontario, Sons and Daughters of American Loyalists of Upper Canada* by W D Reid.

In the UK, there are several printed volumes containing lists of pedigrees including *An Index to Printed Pedigrees* by Charles Bridger and *The Genealogists Guide - An Index to Printed British Pedigrees*

Opposite: Initiation into the order of Knighthood - every young squire's dream come true when he attained his spurs and his armour. Many such knights went overseas to fight in the Crusades on the continent.

Celtic designs carved into Scottish gravestone in the Kirkyard of Kenmore, Perthshire relating to the Revd. Allan Sinclair MA minister of the Church of Scotland at Kenmore and his wife, Sarah. Note the biographical details included in the inscription.

and Family Histories by Geoffrey Barrow. The Society of Genealogists in London has an excellent selection of reference books on printed pedigrees.

Church of Jesus Christ of Latter-day Saints - Family History Centres

Often abbreviated to LDS and also known as Mormons, the members of this faith usually have Family History Centres attached to their main churches, spread all over the world. Their headquarters are in Salt Lake City, Utah, USA where the followers of Brigham Young settled and founded their main church. One of the tenets of their religion is the tracing of their family's ancestors and it is for this reason

Opposite: Excellent example of Monasterboice high crosses and roundtower from County Louth, Ireland. Note the elaborate carving on the stones.

A village inn c.1860. Often the focal point of village life after the church, these inns would provide refreshment to both local people and travellers seeking a bed for the night.

Cambridge University c.1842 - the Senior Wrangler presented to the Vice Chancellor. Such ceremonies are well documented and often depicted in paintings. Records of the students who attended the various colleges have also been published in books along with histories of the famous colleges for both Oxford and Cambridge Universities.

that their records are so helpful to other researches of whatever color, creed or nationality. Their Family History Centres are open to the general public, free of charge. The LDS members produce many helpful aids for family history, the most well known being the *International Genealogical Index* (IGI) - an index to births, baptisms and marriages on microfiche by county and country covering the period approximately 1550-1880, for the whole of the world. The sources from which this index is compiled are mainly church and chapel parish registers and family trees submitted by members.

However, the IGI is only one small part of the material available through the LDS Family History Centres and by using their catalogues and large computer resources, it is possible to check what other records have been filmed. The *Locality Catalogue*, which is divided into country/state, shows all printed material available on film or fiche covering national, federal and local government records as well as privately published records for that particularly place. It is then possible to order copies to be sent to the local LDS centre for viewing there for a small fee.

Most LDS Centres also allow access to their huge computer system which is linked to their headquarters in Salt Lake City. The latest system is the 'Family Search database' which contains genealogical information taken from many different sources including the IGI and Ancestral File, and accessed by merely entering in the name of the family you are seeking. Print out facilities for these and many other LDS records are normally available.

There are many more records held by the LDS centres and these will be mentioned later.

Religious Societies and Church Groups

All over the world different religions have their own customs and tenets. Whether you belong to a Church, Chapel, Temple, Synagogue or Mosque you will find that within your group there are members will be able to advise you on where to seek church records as well as those whose memories may go back two or more generations and who may have information about your particular family's back-

Village school, Somersham in Huntingdonshire, England. Originally built in the 1740s as the school for children of the village, it is now used as a private home. The inscription stone over the doorway gives details of the foundation of the school.

ground that cannot be duplicated elsewhere. It is always worth checking with the local religious societies and groups to see whether any of your family may have been members.

Family History Societies and Groups

Finally, it is important to seek out a local genealogical or family history group. These meet regularly, usually produce a newsletter or periodical in which you can advertise the names you are seeking and will be able to offer guidance on tracing your family and assistance when you meet with problems. The address should be available from the local library. A list of the main genealogical societies is included in the appendix.

If the name you are seeking is unusual or your ethnic group is small and you wish to make contact with others of the same name or group, then you may consider starting your own *One Name* group by advertising in family history magazines. This will bring you into contact with other people with a similar interest with whom you can exchange information and, at the same time, build up a large database of information on the name or group.

Family Crests and Arms

If your family has a motto, crest or family shield it may well be that they were entitled to bear arms, granted by the sovereign of the country at that time. The right to bear arms was awarded to an individual and their descendants, not everyone else who also bore the same surname. The recording of the right to bear a coat of arms, abbreviated to arms, dates in Britain back to the 12th century and, although it is certain that knights used distinguishing devices before this time, the College of Arms was not founded until the mid-1100s. It is assumed that the devices were used to distinguish mounted knights in battle when closed helmets made identification impossible without some outward sign or symbol. The most obvious places for these were on

War memorial on roadside near the disused Polebrook airfield, Northamptonshire, England, commemorating the 351st Bombardment Group of the Eighth US Airforce who were stationed at Polebrook. Such memorials are to be found all over the East of England.

the helmet, shield and surcoat of the knight. The placing of the symbols on the front and back of the knight's clothing gave rise to the term 'coat of arms'. Most of the early designs were simple, often a pun on the owner's name or home place. Thus a knight from Tunbridge might feature a bridge and a tun (a barrel) on his shield. As a general rule, the simpler the device, the more likely it is to be a sign of ancient lineage.

All big reference libraries and genealogical societies hold books on heraldry from all over the world and it is possible to check a known design against pictures in these books to see whether they refer to your own family. If the family line originated in England or Wales, then the College of Arms in London will be able to provide detailed information after a search of their records. The Chief Herald of Ireland's Office is responsible for Irish coats of arms and The Court of Lord Lyon holds those of Scottish families.

The Field Trip

Nothing can compare with standing on the spot where your ancestors stood, many years before, and looking around trying to see the place through their eyes. Visiting the old home area can be both exciting and rewarding.

Whilst collecting information from your relatives on the family history you will, inevitably, need to travel to meet with some of them, often going out of county. It may be that in some cases you are returning to the original homesite of the family, before more recent generations spread out over the countryside. It is always worth taking some time to plan these visits carefully to maximise the benefit.

If at all possible, find out where the family worshipped and pay a visit. You may be able to gain access and see the place where your ancestors were baptised or named or perhaps the place where your grandparents were married. Some religious houses permit photography but always check first.

Graveyards and cemeteries are not everyone's ideal place for a visit

Upwood Parish Church in Huntingdonshire, England. This church, mentioned in the Domesday book of 1086, is dedicated to St. Peter and is typical of a small village church, much loved and used by the community for over eight centuries.

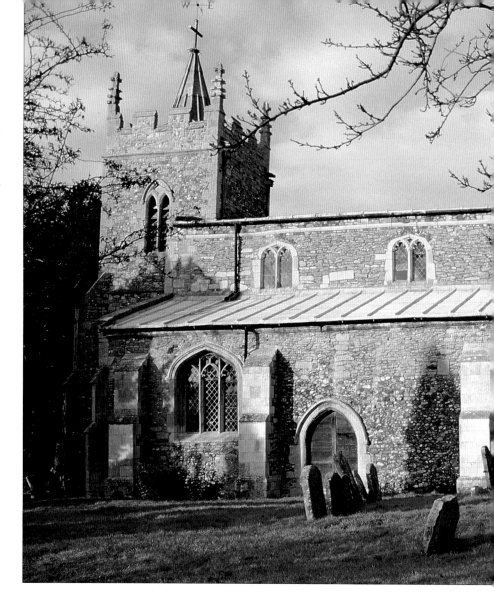

but they must rate very high on the list of places to browse for the family history researcher. Many cemeteries have been catalogued and mapped so it is worth checking first in case there is someone at hand who can show you exactly where your family graves are situated. You may find tombstones or monuments to family members, some of which may even give birth dates and country of origin if from abroad. Watch out for multiple occupancy graves. Where a mother died in childbirth, the infant often succumbed as well and the two would usually have been buried together.

Gravestones in Scotland are particularly informative often naming whole families that left the country for America or Australia in the 1800s. Many of these monuments were erected by members of the same family returning home many years after the burial of the deceased.

European gravestones often contain photographs of the deceased and a biographical precis which can be fascinating.

Do not forget to look out for the school which your family attended as children as well as visiting the local inn where your ancestors may have had a relaxing drink. Take a walk around the area looking out for other sights with which your family would have been familiar in the past.

A large scale map of the home area is also a useful tool to have with you for it will give details of historic houses, inns, churches, roadways and rivers and sometimes even give field and plot names.

Many publishing houses now produce historic maps dating back to the early 1800s or before which show the original settlements. A collection of these maps, made over the years, can help to chart the growth of an area and can explain why a family may have moved - to make way for a major road or housing development.

Remember to take a camera or video recorder with you to capture and record the family members and their treasures. It may not be possible to take great-uncle Tom's collection of family portraits away with you but you can perhaps photograph them.

Finding an old family home when the family have left can always be difficult, especially if the area has undergone development. It is always worth checking with the local library to see whether they have any local plans of the area and any street directories. As a rule, government buildings have tended to remain as such and these can be used as pointers to help identify an old address on a new map. A quick check of a local trade directory or the electoral rolls may also help to pinpoint your family's address. Telephone directories will also help you get in touch with other people of the same surname in the area who may be related.

Where whole areas have been redeveloped, such as in cities like London and Berlin, the city archives departments will have old street plans together with lists of streets that have been renamed and should be able to assist you locate the correct area even if the building has long gone.

Using Official Records

O nce you have exhausted all the local sources of information and gathered together all the information from relatives, you will need to look further afield.

The most useful records to start with will be those termed 'official records' which are, in the main, government, federal or state records.

Right: Copy of Death Certificate for Ada Bradford from Flint, Co. Genesee, Michigan, USA dated 1917. Note that this certificate gives the names and birthplaces for both parents of the deceased as well as the deceased's exact age.

Below: Original Birth Certificate for Nicolas Julian Wright dated 1943. This example clearly shows the wealth of information available from an English birth certificate from 1837 onwards.

Right: Copy of Marriage Certificate for Samuel Wilkinson and Sarah Jane Kettle dated 1878. This couple married at the local Methodist Chapel with the Registrar in attendance. The date printed at the bottom of the certificate shows that this copy was purchased in 1990.

Civil Registration

Civil Registration or the official recording of birth, marriage and death can be one of the most rewarding of the official records to consult. The finding of a birth certificate for the earliest known ancestor in the 19th century can provide a wealth of information about the parents, depending upon where the family were at that time, and can

T—224.

TWELFTH CENSUS OF THE UNITED STATES.

SCHEDULE No. 1.—POPULATION.

State *Michigan*
County *Kalamazoo*
Township or other division of county *Kalamazoo Township*
Name of incorporated city, town, or village, within the above-named division *Kalamazoo City*
Name of Institution,
Enumerated by me on the *1st* day of June, 1900. *Frank E. Evans*

confirm a family line back another generation. Of more interest to Americans and Australians will be the death certificate of their earliest known ancestor since this will give information not only on the date, place and cause of death but also the place and date of birth, nationality and names of parents. Australian death certificates also give the name of spouse, names and ages of living issue, number and sex of deceased issue and length of residence of the deceased person in Australia if immigrant. By comparison, English death certificates are very disappointing, giving only the date, place and cause of death with the age of the deceased.

The commencement date for civil registration varies from country

Copy of 1900 Census Return of United States for Kalamazoo City, Michigan, USA. The various columns show the date of birth, the age, for women, the number of children born and surviving, the place of birth and that of their parents as well as the date and length of citizenship for every individual shown on the schedule.

Copy from 1881 Census Return for St. John parish of Huntingdon town, Huntingdonshire in England. Family relationships are shown and the ages are accurately recorded. The occupations are varied and include an Upholsterer, Hairdresser, Schoolmistress, Nurse, Wheelwright, Basket maker and an Inland Revenue (Tax) man.

to country with national registration in England and Wales starting in 1837, New Zealand in 1848, Scotland in 1855 and Ireland in 1864. In some countries, civil registration records are indexed by town or county such as in France after 1792, Belgium after 1796 and the Australian Capital Territories not until 1930. Most countries started to keep official records of their population's births, marriages and deaths by the mid to late 19th century. Most of the countries that were settled by immigrants, such as Australia and North America, seem to provide more detailed certificates than some countries in Europe, perhaps anticipating the need for future generations to know more about their origins.

The first task will be to ascertain the correct place to contact for your family's birth, marriage and death certificates. For this you will need some idea of where they lived and died. This may vary from generation to generation as the family moved around and split up with children marrying away from home. The next point will be to choose the ancestor to follow further back, whether it is the paternal or maternal line. Try to find out as much as possible about this person, especially their full name and, if possible, some idea of their birth, marriage or death. This will then give you a starting point for using civil registration records. The main point to remember with civil registration is that it is a separate record from any religious ceremony and any index will be based on surname and locality, not religious belief.

The LDS Family History Centres in the USA all hold the Social Security Death Index records for US citizens on microfilm and the help page on this film gives the address of the County Clerk to write to for death certificates in each county across the states.

French and Spanish civil registration records give the names of both sets of parents and the birthplace of the bride and groom on the marriage certificate which can help to track down earlier generations in those countries.

Opposite: Evening Star Green Hawk, a member of the Cherokee nation. These people, together with other native North American Indians, are included in the national US Census Returns.

Mexican Indians performing the "Corn Dance," part of an ancient traditional ceremony.

In England and Wales the registration of births, marriages and deaths is controlled by the Registrar General and the three main indexes for these events are held centrally at St. Catherine's House in London and have been copied onto microfilm/fiche so that they may be viewed elsewhere, in family history centres, archives offices and genealogical centres all over the world. Certificates still have to be purchased through the Registrar General or the local Superintendent Registrar for the district concerned.

Some areas, such as Scandinavian countries, did not have civil registration but used the government-sponsored churches to record the details of birth, marriage and death of the population.

Overleaf: Loch Duich and Eilean Donan Castle, Scotland - much photographed view looking westward out to the Americas where many people of Scottish descent can now be found.

Census Returns

Governments have been recording the numbers of populations since Roman times. These records vary from country to country with the amount of information given and, as a rule, the more recent census returns tend to give the most valuable information for family history researchers. Of particular interest to family historians will be the age of the person on the census and their place of birth. These two statistics can lead back to a birth or baptism and thus to an earlier generation.

In the USA the earliest census return dates from 1790. This showed the name of the head of household, the number of free white males aged 16 years and over, the free white males under 16 years, number

Custer's Last Stand - the Battle of Little Bighorn 25th June 1876. Veterans of this and similar campaigns were recorded on the US Census Returns and family legends of involvement can often be confirmed by consulting such records.

of free white females and all other free persons, the number of slaves, the county and sometimes the town of residence. By comparison the 1900 and 1910 census returns show for each individual the month and year of birth, year of immigration into US, number of years in the US, whether a naturalised citizen, the number of years married, mother of how many children and how many alive at the census date. There is a separate schedule for native Indians for both those living on reservations and those living in family groups outside the reservation. These later census returns have been indexed with Soundex and Miracode respectively which can greatly speed up the finding of an individual within a state. There are many other US census returns such as the 1850-1880 Mortality Schedules.

The 1920 United States census should list the province (state or region) or city of birth for people (or their parents) born in Austria-Hungary, Germany, Russia or Turkey. This can be most useful for more recent immigrants to the USA.

In Australia and New Zealand the census returns have not been kept although there were some early census type records made of the

convicts when they first arrived in Australia.

Canadian census returns prior to 1851 are not particularly helpful, being mostly aggregate (listing numbers rather than names). However, those after 1851 should show the name, age, marital status, occupation, religion, place of birth, nationality, racial origins and education of each individual. There are check lists of census returns available on microform from the National Archives of Canada - see Appendix.

In Great Britain, the census returns were taken every ten years commencing in 1841 and are available to the general public up to 1891, with a one hundred year closure on the more recent census returns. There are no national indexes available, although the Mormons have just completed the indexing of the 1881 British census return onto microfiche, county by county, which is a great finding aid for anyone seeking ancestors in the UK. These fiche are available at all LDS Family History Centres, world-wide.

The 1851 census return has also been partially transcribed and indexed at a local level and it is always worth checking to see

whether the county in which you are interested has published an index. For example, Bedfordshire and Lincolnshire both have indexes for sale and Huntingdonshire has published the 1851 census in book form with the index available on fiche.

The census returns in England and Wales from 1851 through to 1891 give a standard amount of information - the name of the householder and all the people in the same dwelling, showing their relationship to the head of the household, the age and marital status of all persons, their occupation and place of birth. The 1841 census return unfortunately only gives names of groups by dwelling house with no relationship shown, only an approximate age within five years for adults and no place of birth, just confirmation of whether or not born in the same county. A separate column was given for recording whether born in Scotland, Ireland or Foreign Parts/Overseas.

Spain and France took some early colonial census returns in North and South America, some of which contain more detail than others. The records should be in the former colony but may have been retained by the mother country.

Census returns also exist in countries in Scandinavia, Africa, Asia and Latin America but they do not have any national indexes to assist with tracing people. It is necessary to know where the family were living in a census year in order to track them down. Many of the census returns cover small areas and it will be necessary to locate the archive centre holding the appropriate records.

One word of warning when using any census return records. It is worth remembering that when these returns were first introduced, the population would have been very suspicious of the motives behind the government and thus, some of the information given on the census returns may be misleading. Some older people may not have remembered exactly where they were born and may have given the name of a nearby town or just the state name. Some may not have been able to work out when they were born - not all our ancestors

Above: Charles I of Great Britain. The monarchy was restored in 1660 following the Civil War of 1640.

Opposite: General U.S. Grant at his headquarters dated 1864. Records for the soldiers of the civil war can be found in local and national archives and in printed histories.

could read and write and many had to rely upon the enumerator who collected the form to complete the data for them. It was in this way that names were incorrectly recorded, the person filling in the form writing down what they heard and the speaker, not being able to read, could not tell whether the information was being accurately written. Foreign sounding names were especially difficult. Many immigrants altered their surname to fit into their new country, dropping endings of names that sounded 'foreign' or translating the name completely so that Leblanc became White. Be especially cautious with foreign birth places. Where an ancestor has put 'Berlin, Deutschland' they may not actually mean Berlin but the area around the city. Similarly watch out for place names that are common in one country. At the last count, there were fourteen places in Great Britain named Broughton scattered all over the country.

Military Records

Most families will, at one time or another, have had members who served in the armed forces of their country. It will be necessary to find out when and where an ancestor served in order to trace the appropriate military records. Clues to watch out for are campaign medals, medals for bravery, certificates, war diaries, items of military equipment and souvenirs brought back from the battlefield. Most medals can be identified and some are inscribed with either name and rank or date which can help identify the recipient and the conflict concerned.

Many thousands of men served in the United States army during the 19th century and the pension application papers provide a valuable source for researchers. These records may include name, rank,

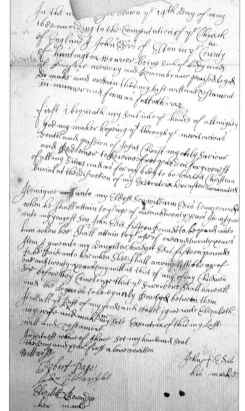

military unit, period of service, residence, age, place and date of birth, marriage and death or nature of disability, if any. The US 1890 census return for war veterans and the 1910 census identify soldiers who served in the American Civil War.

The Spanish military records of about 1790-1805 for Florida, Louisana, the Philippines and Latin American countries were microfilmed in the Archives at Simancas, Spain. They tell much about the soldiers, including their birthplaces in Spain. Many of these men stayed in North America after their New World service. These records have been indexed and printed as *Hojas de Servicios de America*. Many of the original Spanish military records have now been indexed in Spain but, as usual, you do need to know the regiment and company of a soldier in order to find the correct set of records.

As a rule, very few of the military records in any country are indexed. In Great Britain partial indexes exist for the Chelsea Royal Pensioners, whose historic red uniforms are instantly recognisable. In other cases it is necessary to know the regiment in which your ancestor served. The *Index to War Deaths* (held by the Registrar General with indexes at St Catherine's House, London) for the Boer, First and Second World Wars and the Korean War show the name, rank and regiment for the deceased soldier which can help to track down a military record. Much work is being undertaken to index the discharge records held at the Public Record Office in Kew and a check should be made on the progress of this project before embarking upon a lengthy search of military records. Most of the military records for Great Britain are held at the Public Record Office, Kew, Middlesex. Other records may be found at Regimental Museums and may include war diaries and maps.

There was an army in India which was maintained by the East India Company until 1859. This army consisted of separate divisions of European and Indian troops, which were both officered by Europeans. After 1859 the Company's Indian troops became the Indian Imperial Army. The European Regiments became the Regiments of the Line who, together with the Royal Artillery and the Royal Engineers formed the British Army in India. Service records of European officers and soldiers of the Honourable East India Company's service, together with those of the Indian Imperial Army, are held at the India Office Library and Records in London, England.

Records for British soldiers who fought in the American War of Independence in 1776-1783 are preserved in the Public Record Office at Kew in Middlesex. They include muster books and pay lists for many regiments. However records for those men who were discharged in North America and settled there are difficult to trace. There are some records for the Hessian troops in the PRO at Kew but the muster rolls for the Hessian troops in British pay in North America are held in Germany. The Loyalist Regiment Rolls for Provincial Troops are in the public archives in Canada.

Records for the regular army in England and Wales only date from the 1660s after the restoration of the monarchy with King Charles II. Records for the two opposing armies during the English Civil War are patchy and most have been published in book form. There are

Opposite top: Inventory of Goods and Chattels of John Edis of Elton, Huntingdonshire dated 1682. This inventory accompanies the will of John Edis and gives a list of his personal belongings in and around his house.

Opposite left: Will of John Edis of Elton, Huntingdonshire dated 1682. John Edis was a weaver by trade and in his will he leaves legacies to his two named sons and daughter as well as his wife, whom he makes executrix.

Opposite below right: The Quadrangle, Somerset House, London - this building is now used to house, amongst other records, the probate records for England and Wales from 1858 onwards.

some very interesting published collections of letters and diaries from the period held in the Cambridge University Library, England.

Records for the militia in England predate the regular army but are most useful for the period 1790-1816 when Great Britain was at war with France. There was a great fear that Napoleon would invade and, to counter this, regular musters of militiamen, of supplies available, as well as surveys of transport available and local trades people, such as bakers and millers, were made to ensure that a swift evacuation could be made leaving nothing of any value to the invader. These records often show reasons why an ancestor would or could not serve in the local militia are held at a local level within the county concerned and also at national level at the PRO, Kew.

It was also possible to pay for a substitute to take your place, provided you had sufficient funds. Records for these substitutes are held with the militia papers.

Naval Records

Naval records vary from country to country and should be sought in the national archives. It is unlikely that every sailor will be mentioned

A dramatic oil painting by Thomas Chambers, depicting the American Frigate, *United States* capturing the British Frigate, *Macedonian* in the War of 1812.

but it should be possible to locate records for officers when they were promoted, retired to pension or died. The Naval Lists for the British Navy are particularly useful for those seeking British naval ancestors. Background reading on naval encounters for the country concerned will help identify the ships involved and the dates which can then lead to further research in the original records. Check what records are already in print and what official documents have been indexed and published.

Probate Records

One of the most satisfying set of records to consult must be those of probate. The making of a last will and testament is often the last act performed by an ancestor and was their one way of ensuring that their possessions, wealth and estate were distributed according to their wishes after their death.

Most countries have comprehensive indexes for probate records, some at national level, others at state or county level. The probate jurisdictions are usually well defined and maps can be consulted to check as to where to find a particular set of wills. Many of the early

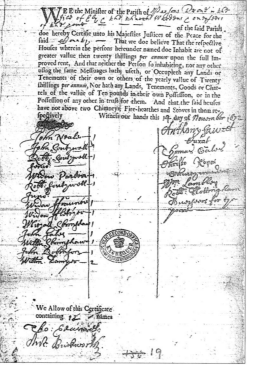

settlers in the USA still held property and estates in Great Britain when they died and the probate records for their wills can provide a wealth of information covering both sides of the Atlantic. Some of these records have been published, such as *English Estates of American Colonists : American Wills and Administrations in the Prerogative Court of Canterbury 1610-1857* by Coldham, available from most large reference libraries and genealogical societies.

South Africa maintained death notices that were included in a deceased person's estate file. These are full of information such as the deceased's place of birth or origin, names of parents and children's names.

One of the problems encountered with probates in foreign countries will be language. Not only will there be the basic language barrier to overcome but the legal terminology may also prove confusing. Most archives will provide copies of probate documents and it is often possible to study the records at home. However, it would be advisable if the records are in a foreign language to consult with a local specialist to ensure that the records, once found, are accurately translated to obtain the full benefit. Local genealogical societies should be able to offer advice.

Fortunately for those people whose ancestors originate in Great Britain, the majority of records for probate after 1550 are written in standard English. However, most of the very early records, dating back to the time of William the Conqueror in 1066, will be in Norman or Court Latin or even French, which was the official language for recording events for some time after the Norman Conquest. Many of these early records have been translated and published.

Probates are invaluable for proving family relationships, father to son, husband to wife, aunt to nephews and nieces and brother to sister. The wills for single people are often of more value than those of married couples since

Above: Copy of Land Tax for hamlet of March, Isle of Ely in Cambridgeshire, England dated 1798. This assessment schedule shows owners of land and the occupiers together with the amount assessed for payment. This clearly written list can provide evidence of whether an ancestor owned the land he occupied.

Right: Copy of Hearth Tax for Parsons Drove, Isle of Ely, Cambridgeshire, England dated 1672. This exemption certificate lists those householders who due to poverty were exempted from paying the tax. The 1672 Hearth Tax was one of the rare occasions when paupers were shown in such taxation records.

the unmarried person may have no direct blood descendants to whom to leave their estate. They usually mention siblings and nephews/nieces, parents and even grand-parents. Property mentioned in such wills can often be traced back to a previous generation and may re-appear in future generations, thus providing a further link within a family's history.

When neither husband nor wife leave a will, local laws will intervene and the property and personal possessions will be divided amongst the next of kin according to custom. In these circumstances, one or two people are normally appointed to supervise the distribution of the estate and the records thus created can provide valuable evidence of family relationships. In England and Wales these are called letters of administration.

One other important set of records relating to probate are inventories. These are lists of a deceased person's possessions, valued at the date of their death by two or more independent assessors, and used to calculate the probate duty. They can provide a wonderful insight into the personal possessions of a long-dead ancestor, and their commercial value. When the home was carefully catalogued it is almost possible to imagine a walk around the dwelling house and envisage the rooms with their furnishings. Certainly some idea of the size and standard of accommodation can be gleaned in this fashion.

When seeking probate records, always start at national level and work down to the local level. In England and Wales, probates from 1858 onwards have been indexed nationally and are held at Somerset House, London where the calendars (annual indexes) can be consulted free of charge during opening hours. The probate documents can be ordered for viewing and copies provided for a small fee. Before 1858, probate was handled by the Church of England under three levels of court. The local level was the Archdeaconry Court. The next level, which covered a Diocese was the Consistory or Bishop's Court. Records for both of these courts will be found at a local level in the relevant county record office. The third and highest court was the Archbishop's Court. There were two, Canterbury and York, Canterbury having precedence over York. The records for the wills and administrations proved at the Prerogative Court of Canterbury (PCC) are held by the Public Record Office in London and those for the Prerogative Court of York (PCY) at the Borthwick Institute in York. Both these sets of records have been indexed but not all the indexes have been published. It is probably worth remembering that if your ancestor died in a foreign land or at sea, still in possession of estate in England and Wales, then details of the probate will be found in the PCC indexes.

Huntingdon Quarter Sessions 1830 - an extract from the printed transcript giving a precis of the various documents contained within the particular Session. Note the large number of bastardy bonds - often the only place to find evidence of paternity for an illegitimate ancestor - as well as the presentment of Thomas Wade of Stilton who was found guilty of his strange antics.

Taxation Records

Governments the world over levy taxes from their citizens to fund the running of the country. Records of payment, or even non-payment, can provide vital evidence of an ancestor's whereabouts at a given time as well as giving some indication of their comparative wealth.

Different countries have different taxes. For example, the *Ireland Householders Index* helps locate families in Ireland between 1820 and 1860 when the census returns are lacking. In England and Wales, the Land Tax which dates from the 1700s right up to the mid-20th century shows the amount of land held, the occupiers of the same land, its whereabouts and the amount paid. An earlier tax, the Hearth Tax, which dates from 1662 to 1689 shows the number of hearths (fireplaces) within a dwelling and the amount paid. This particular tax was collected half-yearly and some of the later records have lists of those people who were exempt from payment as their dwelling was too small. From this tax record it is possible to work out roughly how large the dwelling house was by counting the hearths.

Social Security Records

If your ancestor worked in the USA after 1933, they probably had a social security card. The application form which was completed when the form was applied for should contain the town and date of birth. In order to see this application form you will need the social security number which can be obtained from (some) death certificates. Insurance, bank and employment records are other sources for the social security numbers. This is a unique source, peculiar to the USA, brought about mainly by the Freedom of Information Act.

Newspaper Records

Whilst newspaper records would not normally be regarded as 'official', their reports of births, marriages and deaths can provide valuable information on exact dates and places, which can then lead to official records. Where, for instance, there was some query over the cause of death then an Inquest may have been held and witnesses called to give evidence regarding the deceased. Even more illuminating, if somewhat gruesome, can be the reports on murder and accident victims and the newspaper accounts may be the only way to learn the full story. Occasionally there may be artists' impressions or, for the 20th century, photographs of the deceased and their family.

Obituaries can prove the most fascinating reading and many newspapers have catalogued and indexed their obituaries, such as *The Times* in England.

Some English local newspapers can provide useful clues to occupations. They may list licences granted to gamekeepers or to innkeepers in the 1800s. Reports from the Quarter Sessions where prisoners have been sentenced to transportation or, worse, death may contain information not only on the accused but also the victim and their family.

You may even find notices of parents fined for not sending their children to school after the Education Acts of the 1870s. Not all newspaper records concern specific people. Reports on weather conditions, crops - their growth or failure, epidemics and immunisation programmes, results of local agricultural, flower or livestock shows, cricket team fixtures and match results, visits from foreign delegations or reports sent back from groups of emigrants to their home town; all may feature and will give background information essential to understanding the social environment in which your ancestor lived.

Family Vault of Thomas Wm. Woodgate Esq. in Highgate Cemetery, London. A typical example of a Victorian gothic mausoleum, now much neglected. Records for these memorials are preserved by the burial board and cemetery authorities.

Land and Church Records

Property Records

T he recording of ownership of land and the transfer of land from one owner to another and possible leasing or mortgaging of the same land give rise to excellent records that can not only confirm parentage but also establish a family line up and down the generations.

Even if your ancestor did not own the land on which he lived, he may well appear in the records as a tenant paying rent or renewing a lease. There may be records of the crops grown or beasts reared and sold at market. Some land estates will have made provision for widows and children of workers who died, and some may even have provided work for the widows. In some instances, tenants were encouraged to leave the land and emigrate. One such example can be found during the great potato famine in Ireland in the 1840s, when land owners found it easier to help their impoverished tenants to emigrate than feed, clothe and house them. Records such as *Irish Emigration*

Example of early property tenure record - lease of church land in parish of Upwood, Huntingdonshire, England taken from the Vestry Book for the parish church, dated 1745.

Following on from the potato famine, many families were unable to pay the high rents demanded by landlords who did not understand the extent of the disaster and whole communities were thrown out of their homesteads and forced to leave the country.

Lists 1833-1839: Lists of Emigrants Extracted from the Ordnance Survey Memoirs for Counties Londonderry and Antrim by Brian Mitchell can provide names of tenants and the whereabouts of their landholding.

Where a family emigrated and settled in a new country, they might either purchase or be entitled to land, and records may exist for this. The local courts will have dealt with the property transactions and the records may still be held locally. Most of the early settlers in both North America, Canada and Australia/New Zealand have been well documented.

In Switzerland, mortgage records for property have been recorded since 1759 by seigniories (manors) or castellany (castle lands). After the French Revolution this was continued by the Justices of the Peace and from 1841 onwards the conversators of driots reels (real estate). Each volume has an index by surname which can help to isolate an ancestor who raised capital upon his land.

Belgium also has similar records for mortgages for most of the 1800s, held in the state archives. For those people tracing ancestors in England and Wales, property records can be divided into three categories - freehold, leasehold and copyhold. Freehold and leasehold records are not easy to access since the deeds will almost certainly be held by the current owners of the land.

However copyhold tenure (held by virtue of a copy of the entry in the manorial court rolls) which was only abolished in 1927 can provide an excellent source of family history material. These records which relate to the land held by the local Lord of the Manor from the Crown and leased to tenants and date back in some cases to the 15th century. Property that has remained within one family may be traced back, generation by generation, through the court rolls. One word of warning, the earlier records before 1740 will almost certainly be written in legal Latin and few of these early court rolls have been indexed. Nevertheless, a search through the manorial court

Overleaf: Beautiful fields of Connemara, Co. Galway, Ireland - homeland for many immigrant Irish families in America.

records can provide a wonderful insight to your ancestor's way of life. Not only are property transactions recorded, but also minor misdemeanours such as ploughing up common land, letting pigs or cattle stray, not branding your beasts, felling trees or taking firewood without the Lord of the Manor's consent. Fines were levied for such cases and the amounts entered in the court records. Every time the court met, usually once or twice a year, a Jury or Homage was elected from the tenants of the manor and their names are always listed at the commencement of the proceedings. Regular surveys would be made of the estates within the manor and maps drawn up to show the extent of the manor and the tenants' holdings. These records are usually to be found locally within the County Record Office and information on the number of manors within a county can usually be obtained from either the *Victoria County History* or local trade directories.

William Penn's Treaty with the Indians when he founded the Province of Pennsylvannia in 1661. This treaty and others where original settlers purchased land from the native North Americans are well documented.

As property records in England and Wales date back to the Norman Conquest, they can be invaluable in proving a family lineage. Many of the earliest records have been the subject of academic research, published and available at local level. The Feet of Fines, literally the bottom section (foot) of a legal document containing a precis of the contents, for many counties have been published in England and Wales and these record early property transactions from the 14th, 15th and 16th centuries.

Church Records

The religious beliefs of our ancestors are an important part of their social history and they often had a considerable bearing on the type of records available to later generations. Where a state forbade a certain religion, then adherents to that particular religion would be

Extract from the Manorial Court rules for Upwood, Huntingdonshire dated 1770 showing how moles were to be trapped and a fine paid for failure to comply. This was only one of many similar rules which tenants of the Manor had to fulfil.

reluctant to keep records for fear of persecution. A typical example would be the Roman Catholics in England in Tudor times. On the other hand, Quakers who were particularly heavily persecuted, retained excellent records including their sufferings which detail the troubled times and events for their religion in both England and North America.

Whilst many church record-keeping practices varied, most denominations kept good records, once firmly established. This is particularly true in North America, Australia, New Zealand and Canada where groups of immigrant families, often all of the same denomination, might settle in one place and build their own place of worship. As a rule, these groups tended to stay together and religious communities evolved over the years. This is particularly relevant to Sikhs, Hindus and Moslems whose customs and traditions have been carefully preserved. In these cases, much of the history of the religious group may be oral and it would be best to first find the leader of the group and ask for information about the particular family sought.

The golden rule must be to find out where your ancestor worshipped and where the records relating to that particular religion are kept, with the covering dates of the records.

Roman Catholic records tend to be well kept and marriage records, especially those for France and French Canada and immigrant groups from those countries, often give brides' and grooms' places or origin which can take a researcher not just across a country but across continents.

The French Huguenot and Flemish Walloon settlers in Lincolnshire and Cambridgeshire who came to England to assist with the drainage of the East Anglian Fens, England kept their records in French but these have been translated and much research carried out into Huguenot ancestry by the Huguenot Society.

Baptist records can be a great source of information on ancestors. Meeting book minutes often contain not just details of the admission of new members but the exclusion of others for various offences, notably fornication, adultery and intoxication. New members from outside groups are often noted and letters of introduction mentioned when members move away to join other churches.

Methodist records tend to be more haphazard. In rural areas the churches often joined to form a circuit with several lay preachers travelling around, usually by horseback or in a horse-drawn conveyance, carrying the registers with them. If the weather was inclement or there was an accident, the records may well have been damaged or even lost.

The Society of Friends, (also known as Quakers) is a religious com-

Interior of Old English Cottage c.1750. Labourers cottages often consisted of no more than two rooms downstairs and two upstairs where the whole family would sleep head to toe in large box beds.

munity. It exists in order to worship God and to witness those insights (whether on issues of peace, race relations or social justice) which it has found through its experience of corporate search. The Society has, throughout its history, sought to be meticulous in the keeping of records and recognises that it stands as trustee in relation to these records.

Quakerism arose in the East Midlands of Britain in the late 1640s and spread quickly. Between 1655 and 1662 about sixty Quaker missionaries arrived in North America. Their main centres of activity were New England, New Amsterdam (later New York) Long Island, Maryland, Virginia and the West Indies. A number of Friends developed financial interests in East and West New Jersey and in 1682, William Penn's constitution for Pennsylvania was adopted.

Records for Quakers are well catalogued, especially their monthly meetings where births, marriages and burials were recorded. Because of their reluctance to swear oaths, they were often ineligible for official posts and records exist of court cases where Quakers fell foul of

Overleaf: It is most unlikely that anyone tracing their ancestors could go back as far as the days when Druids held sway at Stonehenge, the mysterious and ancient place of worship in the English county of Wiltshire.

John Wesley - famous founder of the Wesleyan Methodist religion. Extremely popular in 19th-century England, the Methodist movement gathered momentum in the rural areas where preaching circuits were organised with a series of mobile preachers who would travel from village to village, preaching as they went.

the law for non-attendance at church or for refusing to remove their hats or swear oaths of allegiance.

Members of smaller religious bodies, such as the Mennonites and Doukhobors, moved in large groups from specific locations within Europe to settle in new countries. When original church records for these groups cannot be found, there will often be help available from printed histories.

Jewish ancestors

Much has been written about the history of the Jewish people, their expulsion from some countries and flight to others and about their beliefs and customs. A knowledge of this background history is very necessary in tracing Jewish ancestry and the researcher must accept that it may not be as easy for him as for his fellow researches whose ancestors have more, or less, stayed within the confines of one country.

For those people tracing Jewish origins, the place to start must be

Opposite: Page from the Ramsey Psalter dated 1303-1316 : beautiful example of monastic artwork using vibrant colours to depict historical religious events. These Psalters were the earliest form of illustrated book and even those unable to read the Latin text could learn from the glorious pictures. Many monasteries became famous centres of learning with immense libraries of rare books.

'The word of the Lord came to me, saying 'Cry woe to the bloody city of Lichfield'' - George Fox one of the founders of the Quaker movement preaching in the 1600s. This religion, which crossed to the colonies in North America, was much persecuted by the established Church and Government and brought much suffering and hardship to its followers.

Opposite: Utah in mid-west America. Was this what the new settlers had expected?

with the synagogue records and with other members of the same congregation. Much of the history of the Jewish people was learnt by rote and stories or legends can often help track down ancestors who came and settled in a country. Records of trade such as directories, freemen's records and court records may all contain useful information. Jewish people settled all over Europe. There was a prosperous and well-documented community in Holland in the 1600s and if your ancestors were Sephardic Jews from that country you may be able to trace them back to Spain and Portugal whence Jews were expelled in the 1490s. Records of the Inquisition there have enabled a few families to trace even further back. German records may well go back to the 1700s whereas the records of Eastern Poland and Russia may enable you to get back to ancestors born in the late 1700s. Jews were banned from England until the 1650s when Oliver Cromwell permitted some Sephardic Jews to establish a synagogue in London.

There was a mass emigration of Jews from Europe between 1880 and 1914, caused by the severe persecution in Russia and Romania.

Right: Page from baptismal register for Upwood parish church, Huntingdonshire, England dated 1580 showing entries in Latin. Note that each year starts and ends on Lady Day in the month of March. The earliest church registers date from 1538 but many only commence in the mid-late 1500s.

Above: Marriage entries from the parish registers for Upwood church, Huntingdonshire, England dated 1852. Note the occupation of the bride's and groom's father. The Hussey family were, at that time, Lords of the Manor of Upwood

In the 1930s many more thousands of Jews emigrated from Austria and Germany. Many of these emigrants were poor and if they had any possessions would have sold them to raise funds for the fare to their new country. Those Jews who were well established in the new country swiftly set up charities for the benefit of their brethren. In England the Jewish Board of Guardians was founded in 1859.

There are a fortunate few, such as the Rothschilds, who may have descended from rich European merchants or bankers and whose families have been well documented. There was much intermarriage between this 'cousinhood' of six or seven families. There were also families, also well documented, who produced rabbis, teachers and scholar. They had learning rather than wealth.

Many books have been written about Jewish research, amongst which are *Finding our Fathers: a guidebook to Jewish genealogy* by Dan Rottenberg, *First American Jewish families : 600 genealogies 1654-1977* by Malcolm H. Stern ; *Australian Genesis: Jewish convicts and settlers 1788-1850* by J S Levi & G F J Bergman and *The Jews of South Africa from earliest times to 1895* by Louis Herrmann. The Society for Jewish Family Heritage in Tel Aviv, Israel exists to strengthen the consciousnes of belonging to the Jewish People and its spiritual heritage and has published several books to aid researchers.

One of the major problems with researching Jewish ancestry must be

the naming patterns. Surnames were not used as a general rule and it was not until 1787 that Austria-Hungary insisted upon permanent family names and other European states followed soon after. Thus many European Jews suddenly had to find surnames and stories are told of Rabbis reading passages of the Old Testament, allocating names to the congregation as they were read out. Others may have taken the name of the house in which they lived. When they moved, they were known by the name of their previous house which then became a surname. In some cases they may have been descended from one of the old 'Houses' so that Benjamin ben David became Benjamin David which in turn may have changed to Davis. Similarly the 'House' name of Levi was changed to Levy, Lever, Lewin and even Lewis.

The records for male circumcision which may give details of birth and parentage are not usually retained by the synagogue but by the mohel (circumciser) and do not, therefore, have the importance or value of church baptismal records. Some may have been officially deposited.

Marriage may be performed at the synagogue or in a private house, tavern or coffee house. Marriage certificates, after the commencement of civil registration, usually state the place of the marriage which can be helpful in tracking down family members and friends.

Burial has to be carried out within thirty-six hours of death and is following by an official period of mourning lasting seven days, known as the 'sitting shivah'. Local newspapers may carry a notice advising of such a sitting shivah and give the name and address not only of the deceased but of the relative who inserted the notice.

The *Jewish Yearbook* and *Jewish Chronicle* are both excellent sources of information and the Genealogical Society of Utah also

The London Orphan Asylum, Watford. Before the formation of official orphanages, such as Dr. Barnados, orphans and waifs were sent to large asylums and put to work as soon as they were old enough.

Above: Settlement examination for Mary Dovey showing her birthplace was America. The document is dated 1826 and Mary claimed she was aged 45 years old. The text gives a potted history for Mary including the details of her marriage and subsequent movements.

Right: Child labour in a factory c.1853. When times were hard for large families in England and Wales many families sent their young children out to work. It was not until the late 1850s that regulations came into force restricting the age of children and the hours which they worked.

have large holdings of Jewish records for the whole of the world, including copies of synagogue records.

English ancestors

Many of the early settlers in North America, Australia, Canada and New Zealand as well as families living in Great Britain will find that their ancestors originated in England and Wales. There are many books available on researching in Great Britain and the notes below are guidelines only. All of the records mentioned should be found at local level, rarely at the church concerned, but at the local County

PARISH OF *Upwood*		
If excused, write the word "excused". 3.	NAME OF OCCUPIER. 4.	NAME OF OWNER. 5.
	Fairly Thomas	*R.H. Hussey Esq.*
	Bradshaw Charles	*Elizabeth Clark*
	Isley James	*Samuel Lindsell*
	Wheatford Widow	*Self*
	Allpress Joseph	*Catherine Wheatford*
	Julin John	*John Julin*
	Mackness Frances	*R.H. Hussey Esq.*

Above: Page from the Poor Law Rates Book for the parish of Upwood, Huntingdonshire dated 1860 showing the names of owners and occupiers within the village, together with a description of the premises. These rate books can be used alongside census returns and Land Tax records.

Left: Two barefoot Barnado children gaze pensively into their uncertain future.

Record/Archives Office.

The Church of England parish registers officially commenced in 1538, although few actually date from this time. It was not until 1599 that Queen Elizabeth I passed an Act of Parliament enforcing the keeping of parish registers in a specific book and the sending of a copy of the annual registers to the local Bishop. These copies are known as Bishop's Transcripts and usually cover the period 1600 - 1850. They can provide a valuable back up for occasions where the original registers are missing or damaged.

Parish registers provide a record of baptism, marriage and burial. Baptism usually followed birth but occasionally, especially in remote

Glencoe, scene of the famous massacre. Following the uprising of 1745, many clans split apart and, with the introduction of sheep farming on a large scale which deprived the cottager and crofter of their livelihood, many Scots left their homeland to settle overseas, most of them in Canada and USA.

rural areas, groups of children of varying ages from one family may be found baptised together on the same day. Where a child was born illegitimate the parish clerk might enter the baptism as 'child of God' or 'baseborn' and if the father was known then he might also add the phrase 'reputed child of ...'. If this sort of entry is found, then it may be worth checking to see whether the father was made to provide for the child. Bastardy Bonds and Filiation Papers may give a full account of the father's responsibility, detailing his name, abode, trade or occupation and sometimes his marital status.

After 1754, printed Marriage Books were used to record not just the details of the marriage but also the calling of Banns. Where the couple were from different parishes, then the Banns had to be called in both parishes and the Banns book can help locate marriages when they occurred in the other parish. It is in the marriage book after 1754 that you may find the first official signature of your ancestors as they signed their marriage lines. Many counties have published marriage indexes and Boyds Marriage Index covers most of England and Wales.

Burial usually swiftly followed death, the exception being when an Inquest had to be held. It was not until the printed burial registers of 1812 came into force that the age of the deceased had to be entered although some clerks may have added the age of the person before

that date. Where a burial entry states 'From the Union' or 'From the Workhouse' this is an indication that the deceased died in the union workhouse and further details of the death and the admission of the deceased to the workhouse may be obtained from those records.

Care of the poor in England and Wales was the responsibility of the Overseers of the Poor of each parish up to 1834, after which date union workhouses were formed and run by local government. The records of the Overseers of the Poor can provide valuable information on the plight of orphans, for whom homes would have to be found and clothing provided, and also widows who would have received regular relief. These records can also give an insight to the cost of living at that time, with the price of shoes, staple foods and clothing all being given.

In some instances, a pauper might request assistance from the parish only to be turned away as they were unable to prove that they were entitled. The Overseers of the Poor had to ensure that only those paupers who could claim settlement in a parish received parish relief. If they felt that a particular pauper was not entitled because they had recently moved in or were begging from door to door, then they would go before the local Magistrates with a settlement examination and the pauper would be questioned as to their personal history. Records of these settlement examinations can reveal the life histo-

'The Hope Beyond' - a family group gathered on the shore waiting for the emigrant ship that will take them and all their worldy possessions over the sea to a new home.

ry of an ancestor including place of birth, education or apprentice-ship, marriage and children and current occupation, if any. If the pauper could not prove that they were entitled to relief, then they would be sent back to their last place of settlement, usually their home parish, with a removal order. These could take them across the country and, in some cases, overseas to Ireland.

The Church Wardens were responsible for the physical upkeep of the parish church, the maintaining of the church records and the appointment of minor officials. Their accounts often show payments to local tradespeople for goods supplied and, in rural areas, the exter-mination of vermin. Young lads in the parish were regularly paid for the capture of hedgehogs, sparrows or the collection of kite eggs.

If your ancestor lived and worked in one place for more than a gen-eration or two, he and his family may well feature in one or more of the above records.

Scotland

Records relating to Scottish ancestors are held in Scotland. Civil registration commenced in 1855 and the records are held by the Registrar General, New Register House, Edinburgh EH1 3YT. Copies of many of the parish registers dating from 1700 to 1855 and the Census Returns 1841-91 are also held at this address and most have been microfilmed by the LDS so that they may be seen elsewhere on microform.

Probate and property records for Scotland are held at the Scottish Record Office. It is worth remembering that Scotland's legal system was and still is different from English law, having more in common with the French system. Specialist books, such as *Tracing your Scottish Ancestors in the Scottish Record Office (HMSO)* and *Scottish Local History* will provide excellent advice.

Many books have been published on the emigrant Scots - one exam-ple is *Cargoes of Despair and Hope : Scottish Emigration to North America 1603-1803* by Adams & Somerville which describes the con-victs and indentured servants who, together with criminals who were forced to enlist in private regiments, went to North America.

Ireland

Many of the records relating to family history in Ireland were housed in the Four Courts in Dublin. Unfortunately they were all lost when the building was badly damaged after being seized by the Irish Volunteers in the 1916 Easter Rising. However, many church records did survive and catalogues exist to show the coverage of the remain-ing records. In addition, new records that have come to light over the years and copies of older records are being collected and published and much genealogical material is now available for the researcher in Ireland. The most important thing upon starting research in Ireland is to establish your ancestor's home town or area. This will then lead you to the local records, such as church and property, which will prove as useful if not more so than the census returns or civil egistra-tion records, many of which are lost.

Interior of the Hyde Park Family History Centre, London. This newly refurbished centre situated in West London gives access to all the records held by the Church of Jesus Christ of Latterday-Saints (LDS) Most popular source is the new Family Search computer system which is freely available to the general public at any LDS centre.

Previous pages: Four Courts and River Liffey. Dublin, Ireland - home for the records of Ireland up to the present with those for Northern Ireland from 1927 onwards being held in Belfast.

Stranger in a
Strange Land

If your home is to be found in North America, Australia or New Zealand and you are not of native origins, then it is reasonable to assume that, at some time in the past, your family arrived in your country from overseas and settled there. There are a wealth of records available both in the country of arrival as well as in the country of origin which should help the searcher find evidence of their roots.

Each wave of immigrants brought with them their own culture, language and customs from their home country. In some cases these have slowly been assimilated into the settled country's society. Foreign sounding surnames have been subtly altered to be more easily pronounced by strangers, farming practices have been adapted to meet different climates and soil conditions, new breeds of domestic and farm animal have evolved with interbreeding from new and old stock. To balance this, customs of dress, dance and folklore have been preserved and handed down from generation to generation thus

Italian family seeking lost luggage, Ellis Island 1905.

Opposite: Page from the *Book of Kells*, Ireland - a splendid example of celtic artwork and the sort of icon that many immigrant families would bring with them from their homeland.

ensuring that whilst the outward appearance of the immigrant family may have changed, the ethnic origins can still be traced.

The first settlers in North America were the British, Dutch, Spanish, French and Germans. These early settlers have been well catalogued and societies formed for those who can proudly trace their ancestors back to the first ships to land. It is the later settlers who came during the 18th and 19th centuries to open up the west and tame the interior of the country who are more difficult to trace back to their origins. They were predominately from the UK (England, Ireland and Scotland) but the rest of Europe and Asia soon all contributed to the immigrant influx.

European and American ships, trading the slave triangle between Africa, North America and Europe were responsible for mass transportation of black African peoples, often whole villages at a time, to the plantations in North America and the West Indies and, to a much smaller extent, to Great Britain. Much has been written about the conditions of these slave ships and the plantations where the slaves were sent. Family units were divided with mothers and children separated, so that the children often grew up knowing neither their parentage nor their geographical origins.

Specialist societies exist within both the USA and Great Britain to help descendants of these enslaved Africans to trace their roots. There are many records available, on microform and published, including

The storming of Fort Wagner on July 18th 1863, during the American Civil War of 1861–65.

Opposite: Settlers on the Westward trail, North America 19th century. Wagon train convoys would trek across the country, suffering from the heat and exhaustion in summer, and the cold in winter, as well as surviving raids from native Indians and bands of desperate outlaws.

Opposite: Statue of Liberty - often the first glimpse of America for immigrants, many of whom came to America for the dream of freedom, embodied in the statue.

census returns for plantations and indentures for freed slaves in the southern states, such as Alabama. These can be found at major libraries, genealogical centres and at the LDS Family History Centres all over the world.

Australia was originally discovered by the Dutch who named it Van Diemen's Land but it was James Cook, the British explorer, who settled on what is now known as New South Wales in 1770. The first penal colony was formed in 1786 by order of King George III and in 1788 the colony consisted of 1300 convicts. The transportation of convicts to Australia, sometimes together with their families who travelled as free settlers, continued to 1868 by which time 162,000 convicts had been sent from the UK. Twenty five per cent of these were of Irish origin and five per cent of Scottish. The Gold Rush of the 1850s brought a large influx of free settlers, many of whom came from North America. The latest wave of immigrants in the 20th century to Australia is from Asia.

New Zealand was never a penal colony and the settlers were predominately British in the early years.

In Canada the main immigrant groups came from Great Britain and France with, more recently, China, Ceylon, India and Pakistan.

Below: Ellis Island, New York - famous as the holding island for immigrants into the USA.

IMMIGRANT RECORDS
Passenger Lists

Opposite: Immigrants, Ellis Island c.1891 – waiting to be processed before being allowed into the United States of America.

These offer some of the best sources for documenting an ancestor's immigration. Most immigrants should be sought in arrival lists. However, lists were not kept for every immigrant, some have been lost and others are not indexed.

Immigration lists vary in content and availability, depending upon the time period and port of arrival. Early records seldom give the immigrant's town of origin. They often only provide the immigrant's name, age and country of origin or occasionally the ship's last port-of-call. More recent lists tend to give more information, including the place of origin.

Some governments keep comprehensive lists of arrivals called Manuscript Ship Manifests but these vary from country to country. The United States did not require passenger arrival lists until 1820. Canada did not keep them until 1865 and Australian lists date from 1826. However, some port authorities kept their own lists to comply with local laws.

To find an immigrant on a passenger list, you need to know the immigrant's name, port of arrival and the date of arrival. If you do not know the specific date, you may be able to find it by using a ship arrival list if you know the year of arrival and the ship's name. Sometimes immigrants have kept a souvenir of their voyage over to their new country which may give the name of the ship and the year - such as a postcard, letter or photograph.

Passenger lists for most US ports are indexed, so approximate dates are sufficient for these lists. Unfortunately some ports, such as New York City (1846-1897) do not have complete indexes. Such records are so vast that a more precise date, within a week, is required.

Most early lists (prior to 1820) have been published, especially those for North America including *Irish arrivals at New York 1846-1852*; *Dutch arrivals 1820-1880* and *German arrivals 1727-1808*. Other books to look out for are *Passenger and Immigration Lists Bibliography 1538-1900* and *Passenger and Immigration Lists Index* both by W.P. Filby. The famous Ellis Island immigration records date from 1892 and are an excellent source from which to learn the birthplace of immigrants until 1897 when the indexed immigration passenger lists commenced in New York. However, beware of immigrants who did not speak English or did not know how to spell their names. Many overworked immigration clerks wrote what they heard phonetically.

Information on lists available and printed archives are also available from the national archives of the various countries. There are also some more unusual immigration lists such as the Canadian border crossings to the United States published in the indexed volumes *Rapport de l'Archiviste de la Province de Quebec* under *Conges et Permis* (leaves and permits). Many thousands of French Canadian fur-trappers crossed from Canada to settle in the western and central States of America. Fifteen thousand of these men received permits to travel and work in these area. Most eventually returned to Quebec

but many also settled and married a wife of either European or Indian descent and remained in what is now the United States. These records cover the period from 1681 through to 1821.

Millions of citizens of the United States have Spanish ancestry, especially through Mexico, Puerto Rico and Cuba but also directly from Spain itself. The names of more than eight thousand Spanish immigrants entering via New Orleans between 1820 and 1865 have been published by Charles Maduell. The Archivo General de Indias at Sevilla, Spain has published passenger lists for emigrants from Spain between 1509 and 1701. Most of these records give parentage, age and birthplace and are available on microfilm at LDS Family History Centres world-wide.

In 1849 twenty-one families from Russia came to the United States of America and some settled on Kelley's Island, Erie Co., Ohio. Their leader returned later to Russia and praised his new home so much that a further 300,000 Russians, some of German and Polish descent, left Russia to settle in the USA, South America and Canada. Research into Russian ancestry is becoming easier with glasnost and there are several helpful organisations for researches. *A Handbook of Archival Research in the USSR*, published by Princetown, NJ lists some of the

Above: Newsies, Albany, NY - February 1910. This illustration shows the wide variety of newspapers available locally, each one with its own stories and gossip columns.

Opposite: The Capitol, symbol of American justice and law.

101

Mormon Temple, Salt Lake City. It is near Salt Lake City that the Mormons have their massive storage vaults containing their church records on microform and in print. Tours can be arranged with the Church, and many researchers rely upon the records which can be accessed worldwide.

sources available in the former USSR. The LDS Family History Centres Locality Catalogue shows details of books in print, some in English but mostly in Russian, as well as census returns, church records and land transactions that are available on microform.

German immigrants to the USA are well served with the excellent published passenger lists such as *German Immigrants: Lists of Passengers bound from Bremen to New York 1847-1871* by Gary Zimmerman and Marion Wolfert. Ther are other similar records in existence for Antwerp.

British convicts transported to Australia are well recorded in the published books on the First and Second Fleet and since the recent bicentential celebrations, much work has been carried out by Australian researchers and genealogists to catalogue, transcribe, index and publish material about the early settlers in Australia. such as *The First Fleeters* or the more intriguing *Notorious Strumpets and Dangerous Girls: Convict Women in Van Diemen's Land* by Philip Tardif.

Court Records

In America and Canada, court records may name family members and link them to property deeds. New settlers arriving in the country would register with the court to obtain land grants. Many of the early land grants have been published, such as the *Biographical Dictionary of Early Virginia 1607-1660* by Ransome B. True. Most published records are available on microform through the LDS Family History Centres or genealogical societies world-wide.

More than 50,000 English immigrants to colonial America and 150,000 to Australia were exiled convicts and the local courts tended to watch over them carefully. Any infringement of the law or local custom was recorded.

English court records cover a wide range of events from the licensing of victuallers, examining of bastardy claims, reviewing the state of the highways and rivers and the recording of Roman Catholic dissenters called recusants, through to the more expected records of criminals and petty thieves. One of the more unusual things to be found in English quarter session records are the registrations of aliens from 1792 onwards where foreigners settling in England or Wales had to register with the local magistrate giving his name, address, rank and occupation. Anyone offering accommodation to an alien had to give notice to the local magistrate also.

In some cases it is possible to track down the actual case where an ancestor was transported to the colonies for a minor felony. One such case was that of William May, aged 21 years, a labourer from Huntingdonshire in January 1852. He was charged with having broken into and entering a certain building attached to the dwelling house of Thomas Elgood of St. Neots in the same county, and stolen a quantity of copper pence and half-pence, to the value of six pounds. For this seemingly minor crime, William May received a sentence of seven years transportation.

Court records in England and Wales are generally held by the local County Record/Archives Office and not the courthouse.

Library Archives

Most libraries will contain local studies sections which focus on the cities, towns, counties, regions or subjects they service and whilst some will have a national focus, others may have a strong immigrant or ethnic focus.

Where there is a large immigrant population in one area, ethnic newspapers and radio programmes may be produced. Immigrant groups may form societies which keep records of members and their

homecountry. Printed histories for many immigrant ethnic and religious groups often identify all the members and give details of their homeland. A typical example would be *History of the Tunkers and the Brethren Church* by Henry R. Holsinger.

The Society of Genealogists in London, England holds many records relating to ethnic groups in the UK as well as records concerning emigrants from the UK to both North America and Australia.

The LDS Library at Salt Lake City also has a huge library of material on immigration, including books as well as indexed lists, catalogued and available for viewing mostly on microform.

Published histories of the town or region where your ancestors settled when they arrived may give information about their origins. These will be found in local libraries and often in the local genealogical society. Local histories mention not just the prominent citizens but ordinary folk also and a mention in such a history may well solve the question of your family's origins.

Land and Property Records

Many immigrants left their homelands for the chance to obtain inexpensive land in a new country. Most deeds include details of the buyer's and seller's address. Agents toured Great Britain in the 1800s encouraging farmers and their labourers, craftsmen and skilled workers to emigrate to the United States and Canada with offers of cheap passages and good land. 'Headrights' (the head of the house's right to land for settling a colony) may show places of origin. These records are to be found in book such as *Cavaliers and Pioneers : Abstracts of Virginia Land Patents and Grants 1623-1732* by Nell Marion Nugent.

Land records therefore may contain excellent details about the immigrants even if the country of origin is not given. Information

about the immigrant's old hometown may be found in the records of land purchased directly from the government, such as homesteads, rather than from private individuals.

Some places required that an immigrant become a citizen of the country before buying land. Land records may contain details of naturalization records or dates. A typical Canadian source for such information is *Saskatchewan Homestead Records, 1870-1930, with index* from the Canadian Department of the Interior held on over fifteen hundred reels of microfilm.

Above: Boston from East Boston. Illustrations such as these appeared in local newspapers and magazines to encourage people to emigrate. Often the truth was far removed from the artists' impressions.

Naturalization and Citizenship Records

The process of naturalization or taking up citizenship vary from country to country and also over the years have changed. Early records usually give the immigrant's name, age and country of origin. Some of the more recent records give a wealth of data on the immigrant and his family, including specific places of origin.

Not all immigrants were naturalized. In many instances it was only necessary for the head of the household to apply and the spouse and children all gained citizenship through the head of the household. Naturalization was not necessary if the immigrant settled in a colony of the mother country. Immigrants to Canada up to 1947 were regarded as Canadian citizens without naturalization.

The US census return for 1900 shows whether a citizen was naturalized and the number of years resident in North America.

Opposite: Page from the *Bedford Times and Independent* newspaper for January 5th 1912 showing an advertisement offering 160 acres of land for emigrants to Canada. This style of advertisement was common at this time and many young men took up the offer, settling in Canada just before the outbreak of World War 1.

Making
the Link

Below: Postcards across the ocean – this one sent upon arrival at Rimouski, Canada 1907 gives valuable information. Not only does it show the date of emigration and the name of the ship, but also the addressee in England.

I f your researches have proved that your family were immigrants, then there will come a time when you will need to look at the records for the family in their homeland. For the majority of settlers in Australia and Canada this will be Great Britain. For those people who settled in the USA, this may be Great Britain, Europe, Africa or Asia.

Some of the main problems with transferring researches from your home country to your family's homeland will be distance, language and custom.

Distance, nowadays, is not such a major obstacle. Telephones and facsimile machines make communication much swifter than the days of the pony express. Nevertheless, it is frustrating to wait up to three weeks for a reply to a written enquiry only to learn that you were given the wrong address or department and have to repeat the whole process. It is a good idea to make contact with either a local

Opposite: In some cases it is essential to obtain local help.

Above: Dunster Yarn Market, North Somerset, England - site of the old yarn market, nestling under the castle on the hill. This famous local landmark is excellently described in booklets and free publications available from the Tourist Board, which also sell maps and provide information on places to visit.

Opposite: Cape Cod First Congregational Church, USA. Records of such important buildings will be well preserved and local people will usually have some knowledge of the history of the area.

researcher or family history group near your ancestor's home so that you have someone to help you who is familiar with the records.

Planning a visit to the homeland can turn a fun hobby into an expensive luxury. Nevertheless, it is always worth making the effort if at all possible to visit the family homeland, to walk the same streets, see the same buildings, talk with some of the people whose ancestors would have known yours and to visit the church, chapel, mosque, temple or synagogue in which your family worshipped. Take time to visit the local Archives Centre and seek out information not only about your ancestors but also the community in which they lived. Some travel organisations specialise in arranging trips for people wishing to visit their ancestor's homeland and some genealogical societies arrange for exchange visits between countries.

Language can be a major problem and stumbling block. It is bad enough deciphering our own ancestor's handwriting but reading and understanding the records of a foreign country when written in their language, complete with abbreviations, can deter the most enthusiastic researcher. In these circumstances, it is always worthwhile seeking expert help either in the form of a professional researcher who is familiar with the country and language or from a specialist society,

Above: Foot of stone monument - Mother and Father. Often details of the deceased and their family can be found on curbstones around the grave, but if the site has been neglected over the years these may have crumbled away or been removed, and only the headstone remains.

Previous page: Andris Apse, New Zealand. In some cases your ancestors may have travelled across the world to settle.

such as the Anglo-French Society, organised to promote the research of records in France by English-speaking peoples all over the world. Such societies may offer translation services or recommend agents or researchers who will be able to help. They will also print lists of newly published records and advise members of visits to the homeland.

It is always worthwhile trying to learn a few basic words of the foreign language. You may find that some of the older members of the family still retain some knowledge of the language. Being able to translate church records or census return entries will enhance your enjoyment of the research, even if you have to employ others to obtain the actual documents.

It is the customs of the homeland that can provide the most daunting problems. Once the family have emigrated from the homeland, they will have left behind their culture and roots. Whilst they may have brought with them customs from the old country, these will have changed over the years and may no longer correspond with those still taking place in the homeland. Customs such as baptism or naming of children, celebration of marriage, burial rites may all have altered with the passage of time and distance. It is vital, therefore, to carry out as much research into the background of your family in their homeland before trying to tackle the researches into the family itself. Learning about the history of the homeland, the politics, economics and religious societies can all help to make the research easier when you start on the original records.

Above: Decorative grave memorial to one of the Fellowes family of Ramsey, Huntingdonshire. This style of fanciful artwork was popular in late Victorian and early Edwardian times. Many of the larger London cemeteries are full of such ornate stonework.

Left: Hunting in Greenwich Park, London c.1602. Many of the royal parks and palaces are now open to the general public, including Greenwich, Hampton Park and, most recently, Buckingham Palace. It is now possible to stroll around the gardens once the preserve of the nobility.

The
Finished Article

O nce all the information is assembled and all sources examined for details on the family's history, the next step will be to put it together in some sort of logical order so that other people, family and friends can enjoy the fruits of your labours. Whether or not you keep your information on computer has to be a personal decision and advice should be sought from other individuals who have successfully used different computer software before embarking upon the mammoth task of entering all your family data into a computer. However, most people start with pencil and paper making notes and taking copies of original documents. It is worth noting that most archive repositories do not allow the use of ink pens or biros and a good stock of pencils, erasers and a pencil sharpener should form part of your basic research kit.

Old women rusting out c.1892. The system of Union Workhouses went out of use in the early 1900s and many of the old buildings were turned into hospitals or hostels. Family stories of times in such institutions are valuable oral history that should be recorded for posterity.

Record Keeping

When copying out records or extracting information from original documents, do not forget to number your pages so that, later on you can tell whether a page is missing - not always apparent when you are reading the finished article. Also make a note of the archive reference and the years covered when you start work on any archive. This will help you later when you go back over your notes. You may find that the event you are seeking took place just outside the covering date of the records examined.

It is always a good idea to sketch a quick drop line family tree as you are working - this helps to keep track of the children in each generation and can highlight problem areas, such as too many children in too short a space or a husband with two wives - this would almost certainly indicate two families in the same area with the same set of names. Such sketch trees should be simple, showing the husband and wife or wives if more than one marriage, joined with an '=' sign to denote the marriage. The children are taken from this marriage sign down to the line below and always kept in order of birth with the eldest on the left-hand side. Children of second or subsequent marriages should be taken down from the later marriage sign. These children will be half-brothers and sisters.

When it comes to sorting out the research notes, it will be necessary to complete a personal data sheet for each member of the family. This will contain information on their birth or baptism, marriage, death and burial together with place names and dates, names of children, occupations and sightings on various documents. Family history societies and the LDS Centres all produce printed charts for this purpose and a sample is enclosed. These sheets can be coded to link with a family which becomes the visual guide to progress with the researches.

A family tree can become a work of art when drawn up by a professional calligrapher. There are organisations who specialise in producing such documents which can be framed and should become the focal point for family interest. However, most researchers are quite happy to use either a computer enhanced family tree or a hand-drawn chart which has the advantage of being altered with little

Interestingly illustrated gravestone for the Prosser family of Pentonville, London located in Highgate Cemetery. Such examples of family graves should be photographed and can then be included in printed family histories as well as giving valuable information on the family background.

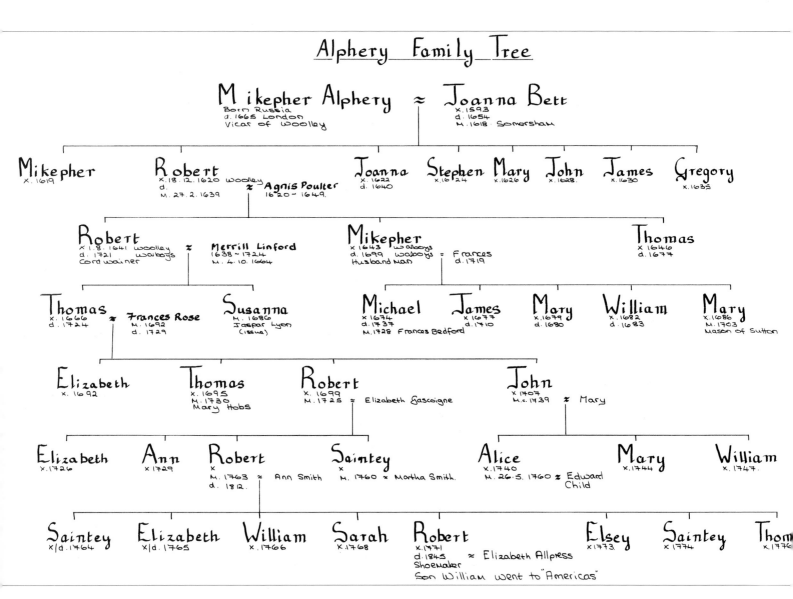

Alphery Family Tree

An example of a hand-drawn family tree, this one of the Alphery Family from 1665 down to 1845. Note the William Alphery, son of Robert, who went to the 'Americas'.

expense if additional information comes to light. Such trees can be drop-line pedigrees showing one family name, carried through from generation to generation, with all the children listed but no maternal lines other than the name of the spouse. They can then be coded to the individual's data chart and a new tree drawn up for each marriage partner.

Other charts show each generation as the parents only, and thus include thirty-two great-great grandparents on one chart. These can, in turn, also be linked to drop line pedigrees where all children are shown for each generation. A sample of such a form is shown.

Booklets such as *Laying out a Pedigree* by Eve McLaughlin can be helpful when first starting to sort out your research data.

Whether or not to publish

The first consideration will be whether to produce just one copy of the family history or whether to supply several copies to members of the family, or even to market the history to outsiders. It is never a good idea to keep original documents in the family history book, but

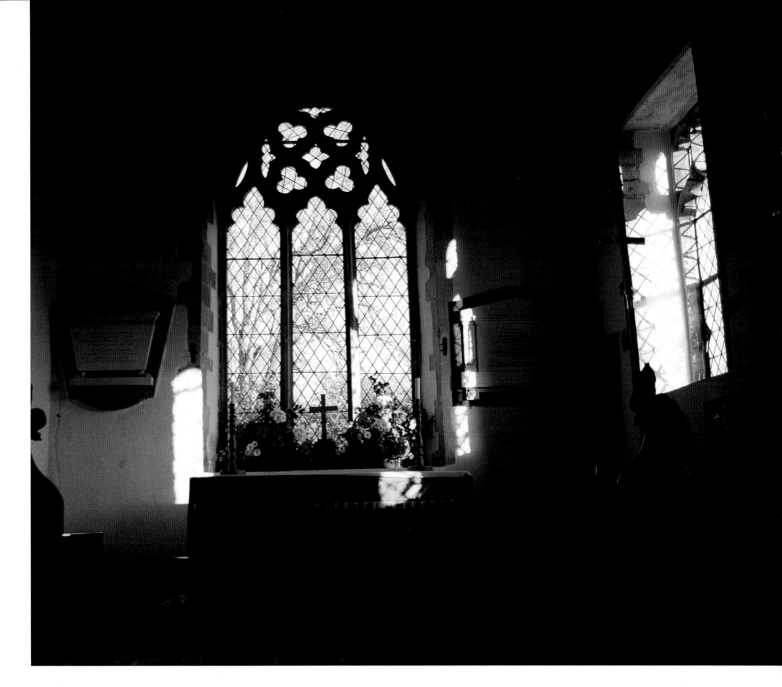

facsimiles especially laser prints can give excellent reproduction of old documents and photographs. Very few family histories will be of any great interest to other people outside the immediate family. The exceptions to this being histories of famous (or infamous) characters in history, royalty and celebrities. It would be rash to rush into print in the hope of producing a best-seller without first checking the potential market.

The family history can either start with the present and work back through the generations or can start with the earliest known ancestor and come forward through time. Whichever method is employed, it is worth leaving a few spare pages to record information that comes to light later on.

Stick only to proven facts and give evidence for each event, be it birth, marriage or a geographical move. It is not sufficient to state that a family left one area to settle in another without producing some evidence and being able to explain why the move took place. If this information is lacking, then perhaps there is scope for further research.

Do not forget to give background information on the area and time

Interior of a village church showing the altar and wall memorials. It is always worth taking a camera when visiting the hometown in case you are able to gain access to the family place of worship.

in which your ancestors lived. What shops did they visit, at which religious house did they worship, where was their home? Include wherever possible photographs or drawings of places and landmarks. However, do beware of copyright laws which may relate to official records.

It is always worth donating a copy of your completed family history to the local genealogical society or the archives office so that other researchers who, in years to come, may enquire about your family name will be able to consult your work.

Many office equipment and stationery stores can provide a copying or printing service upon receipt of a typed manuscript and some will even offer a binding service. This will provide you with copies of your family history to hand out to relatives and friends at a reasonable price.

Employing a Professional Agent

It may not be possible to carry out the researches first-hand and, in these circumstances, a professional researcher can be employed. Most countries have a regulating body for researchers, such as the Association of Genealogists and Record Agents (AGRA) in England, which should guarantee the work of members. Professional researchers usually advertise in genealogical publications such as *Family Tree Magazine* or the *Genealogical Researcher* and it is always worth checking with two or three for details of their terms of business before choosing one agent. However, the best way to find a good and reliable agent has to be by personal recommendation from another satisfied client.

Researches from Home

Not everyone is able to get out of the home and travel to research centres. This need not be a problem for the family historian as much work can be carried out from home. The acquisition of a microform viewer will enable you to purchase or loan from libraries many records that have been copied. The LDS Family History Centres and Genealogical Societies will be able to advise on what is available and many Archive Offices now produce copies of records for sale in microform.

Many official records can only be accessed by written request and much ground can be covered corresponding with other researchers. E-Mail is the latest craze to sweep through the computer world and information can be accessed from all over the world.

Joining local genealogical societies for the areas where your ancestors lived will give you access to other people interested in research who may be able to assist you with one the spot searches and photographs. You will be advised of new publications and local history archives in print. Many genealogical societies also run courses on tracing family history and local history subjects and this can be a good way to gain experience without having to travel any great distance.

Above all, remember that seeking your family roots should be an enjoyable experience that can be shared with all your family wherever they live.

Useful Addresses

Australia

Australian Inst. of Gen. Studies, P O Box 339, Blackburn, Victoria 3130

Society of Australian Genealogists, Richmond Villa, 120 Kent Street, Observatory Hill, Sydney 2000

National Library of Australia, Parkes Place, Canberra, ACT 2600

Canada

National Archives of Canada, 395 Wellington Street, Ottawa ONT K1A 0N3

Archives Nationales de Quebec, Western Quebec, 1945 rue Mullins, Montreal, Quebec

Canadian Federation of Gen. & Family Hist. Soc. 227 Parkville Bay, Winnipeg, MB R2M 2J6

Family History Assoc of Canada, PO Box 398, West Vancouver, BC V7V 3P1

Great Britain

Society of Genealogists, 14 Charterhouse Bldgs, Goswell Road, London EC1M 7BA

Association of Genealogists and Record Agents, 1 Woodside Close, Stanstead Road, Caterham, Surrey CR3 6AU

Federation of Family History Societies, Admin. c/o Benson Room, Birmingham & Midland Institute, Margaret Street, Birmingham B3 3BS

General Register Office, St. Catherine's House, 10 Kingsway, London WC2B 6JP

Public Record Office, Ruskin Avenue, Kew, Richmond, Surrey TW9 4DU

General Register Office Scotland, New Register House, Edinburgh EH1 3YT

Public Record Office of Northern Ireland, 66 Balmoral Avenue, Belfast BT9 6NY

Association for the Study of African, Caribbean and Asian Culture and History in Britain, c/o Inst. of Commonwealth Studies, 28 Russell Square, London WC1B 5DS

Netherlands

Central Bureau Voor Genealogie, POBox 11755, 2502 At The Hague, Netherlands

New Zealand

New Zealand Soc. of Genealogists, PO Box 8795, Symonds Street, Auckland 1035

New Zealand FHS Inc. Mrs J. Lord, PO Box 13301, Armagh, Christchurch

Gen. Research Inst. of New Zealand, PO Box 36-107, Moera, Lower Hutt

Registrar General's Office of Births, Deaths & Marriages, PO Box 31, 115 Lower Hutt

South Africa

Gen. Soc. of South Africa, The Secretary, PO Box 2119, Houghton 2041, SA

West Rand FHS, Mark Tapping, PO Box 760, Florida 1710, SA

United States of America

Family History Department, Genealogical Library, 35 North West Temple Street, Salt Lake City, Utah 84150

The Genealogical Publishing Co. Inc. 111 Water Street, Baltimore, Maryland 21201

National Genealogical Society, 4527 17th St North, Arlington, Virginia 22207-2363

Avotaynu: the International Review of Jewish Genealogy, 155 North Washington Avenue, Bergenfeld, NJ 06621

Miscellaneous

The Anglo-French FHS, 31 Collingwood Walk, Andover, Hants SP10 1PU, GB

The Anglo-German FHS, 14 River Reach, Teddington, Middx TW11 9QL, GB

Guild of One-Name Studies, Miss J Freeman, Box G, 14 Charterhouse Bldgs, Goswell Road, London EC1M 7BA, GB

Huguenot & Walloon Research Assoc. Mrs J. Tsushima, Malmaison, Church Street, Great Bedwyn, Wilts SN8 3PE, GB

Irish Research Society, Mr. R. Findlay, c/o 82 Eaton Square, London SW1S 9AJ, GB

Irish FHS, c/o The Secretary, PO Box 36, Naas, Co. Kildare, Eire

Society of Friends, Friends House Library, Euston Road, London NW1 1BJ

Glossary

Abstract: Abbreviated version of document giving pertinent details.
Ag. Lab: Agricultural Labourer.
Anabaptist: Derogatory term usually applied to Baptists or Quakers.
Annuitant: Person in receipt of a pension.
Archive(s): Historical document or place where kept.
Calendar: Index or abbreviated version of documents.
CRO: County Record Office (Eng & Wales).
Church Warden: Church appointed office responsible for upkeep of church property.
Deposition: Testimony given under oath in a court.
Emigrant: Person leaving a country.
Executor: Person(s) appointed to administer the terms of a will, admistration or trust.
Family History: Study of the social and historical background of a family.
FHS: Family History Society.
GRO: General Register Office (Gt. Britain).
Genealogy: Study of family pedigrees.
Immigrant: Person arriving in a country.
Intestate: Dying without having made a will or testament.
Journeyman: Person whose apprenticeship was complete and who was hired out by the day.
LDS: Abbrev. for Church of Jesus Christ of Latter-Day Saints.
Non-conformist: Person who does not conform to the establishedreligion of the country.
Overseer of Poor: Church appointed official responsible for care of poor within a parish (England & Wales).
Probate: Legal procedure for the official recording of wills, testamants and granting letters of administration
Relict: Widow.
Stranger: Person not a native of the parish.
Yeoman: Often misused, usually denotes man who held freehold land.

Index

Picture Credits

Sonja Bullaty: 8, 11 (top & bottom), 16, 17, 21 (left & right), 22 (top), 23, 29, 31, 31, 36, 37, 38/39, 42 (top & bottom), 43, 46, 54 (top & bottom left), 60, 61, 66 (left), 72, 80, (top & bottom), 82 (left), 83 (left), 88, 104, 108 (left & right), 110, 120, 121.

Library of Congress (USA): 13, 92, 101.

Mary Evans Picture Library: 9 (top), 14, 15, 20, 24, 25 (top), 26, 27, 32/33, 34/35, 53, 66 (bottom), 78, 82 (right), 83 (left), 94, 118.

Bullaty Lomeos: 96, 111.

National Portrait Gallery, Smithsonian Institution/Art Resource: NY: 58/59.

Nawrocki Stock Photo (USA): 30 (liam Finney).

Ronald Pearsall: 9 (bottom), 10, 12, 28, 54 (bottom right), 62/63, 67, 73, 77, 81, 84, 85, 105, 119.

Dan Peha 19: 102.

Pierpoint Morgan Library/Art Resource, NY: 76.

Picture Perfect: 6/7, 18/19, 22 (bottom), 40/41, 45, 46/47, 48/49, 56/57, 64/65, 68/69, 74/75, 79, 86/87, 89, 90/91, 97, 100, 106/107, 109, 112/113, 116/117, 123.

The Board of Trinity College, Dublin: 93.

Nicolas Wright: 42 (middle).

The author and publisher would also like to give thanks to the following organisations and individuals who kindly gave permission for various documents and photographs to be reproduced in this book: the Carter family; Mrs. A. Howe; The Lord De Ramsey; the Archdeacon of Huntingdon; Huntingdon Record Office; Public Record Office, London; the Revd. J. Simpson of Upwood Parish Church and Mr M. Vickery, headmaster of Upwood County Primary School.